THE CLEARING

A BLACK GIRL COLLECTING HER BONES

NAOMI SCHERELLE DAUGHERTY

The Clearing: A Black Girl Collecting Her Bones
© Naomi Scherelle Daugherty 2021

Published by Nine Pages Media
asiarainey@gmail.com
www.ninepagesmedia.com

All rights reserved. This book or any portion thereof may not be reproduced or used in any manner whatsoever without the express written permission of the author.

Cover art illustrated by Charles Chaisson.
Cover based on a photo captured by Shaquille Dunbar.
Back cover photo by Amina Desselle

for black babies born of red dirt and resilience—
remember our skin holds the sun.

She did not tell them to clean up their lives or to go and sin no more. She did not tell them they were the blessed of the earth, its inheriting meek or its glorybound pure. She told them that the only grace they could have was the grace they could imagine.

That if they could not see it, they would not have it.

— *Beloved*, Toni Morrison

{ the clearing }

1	beloved
2	the clearing
4	deconstructed psalm
7	rigor mortis
8	rememory
10	libation
11	roots
13	fire at massa's house
15	possession
18	rumble
19	loud mouth
21	a first time
23	and the godly ones will hear us
25	reaching
31	spirit of discernment
32	loose womyn
34	time
35	wet behind the ears

{ beloved }

by age 12 i was already
a dead daddy's child
a bitch according to grandma
molested
evicted
poor
somebody's burden
a forgotten memory
of my paternal family
bullied
a bully
slit wrist
bleeding
possessed
the ghost of a dead grandmother
spent
depressed

but i was also be-loved.

{ the clearing }

dignified.
we pull whole towns and cities
out from underneath the dust
clamped sacredly between our toes—
pullin' smiles across uneven bones
lacing together severed spines
ripping off rigid practice.

once we held space underneath cocoons,
now we gather and banter
while new moons piss
between our thighs,

we beckoned ourselves here
to await the cleanse.
wetting our mouths
and feet and hands
with our own seeds—
we fertilize ourselves
dignified. in the good
stench of our rumble
kissing our black bones
together. stitching forward
our breast reaching up
calloused hands to touch
sanctuaries of unmerited

sanctified laughter

whole barrows of us
switch, run, and clap
smackingly to paint
our new smiles on such
dignified moons.

praising up our eyes
with affixed bones
and open throats
we sing a peaceful

shout.

{ deconstructed psalm }
after psalms 23

yea, though i walk through the valley of the shadow of death

death sits around me in corners, she seeps and swells into the concrete, tucks herself into the walls, dances on the better side of clouds, pushes secrets into my dreams, pushes me awake with prophecies i yearn to shake from the innocence of my memory.

i will fear no evil;
for you are with me;

when i was nine, death visited me for the first time. ruthlessly but with intention. death blessed me with images of her wrapped around my father, kissing his forehead, warming his back. a warning, a mercy—a gift i did not want.

at nine i shook with sweat on my raw skin knowing that in the morning, death would come.

your rod and your staff, they comfort me.
you prepare a table before me in the presence of my enemies;

death always proves itself villain and hero. she came again the week my father passed to gather up more of my bloodline. my eyes were still wet when my auntie died.

then, death possessed my mother. gave her unhinged thoughts. depression to heal up and resurrect.

grief stayed after that, a persistent heartache, a saturated lullaby.

you anoint my head with oil;
my cup runs over.

i got baptized soon after death came to me for the first time. loss had come to claim more of my freshness, snatch what should have only been mine, and erode cum into a holy space that was meant for diamonds—

so before i learned that my body was a vessel for creation, blessing, universe, restoration—

i learned that it needed to be cleansed. made over. rid of sin.
so i fell into the water, to be baptized.

surely goodness and mercy shall follow me
all the days of my life;

death showed me apple don't fall too far from the tree. so i fell into craziness too: a safe haven, a trance, stillness. at 16 i wanted nothing more than to look death in the eye, gorge at death's doorway, make death meet what she created, become one. i was sure that if i peeled off my brown skin with slick razor blades, i'd prove that i was worthy of death too.

and i will dwell in the house of the lord forever.

in the only church that i've ever called home, i can see death. she's right at the front of the church underneath the place where sometimes preachers sing love songs to god. that place at the front of the church where my father laid cold, black, and dead is also the place where my brother held his wife for the first time. my father, grief, and i were all there feeling and seeing love, knowing and seeing death.

this will be forever.

{ rigor mortis }

i've got turned up cabbages, a torn-out harvest,
and molding at the root.

parasites are making home in me. i had hoped to be left for dead.

instead, they hold me here, trying to revitalize my dead body, trying to detain the hateful haint i'm soon to become. i begin to fade, careful not to drown in puddles of my own quick fear, careful not to enjoy this too much. i may climax as the sugar in my mouth crusts over, i may snatch this chance at ecstasy; get high on it, as what is left of my spirit pierces into holiness and denies these ravished bones.

i can see the high and holy folks frowin' at me
throwin' pissy looks at my smile.

{ rememory }

ancestors don't always come in whispers
they don't always tuck kindly in corners
laced with rosaries
sometimes they come reckoned and
reckless with ribbons tied to their tongue,
vengeful with slingshots
wrapped 'round their thighs
haughty with the finest type of
rebuke, they come steady handed
and worthy—

my ancestors bear salt on their tongues
lift rocks and waters and make them cry out
these rocks and my ancestors know the name
they gather and become god
my ancestors make those who pillaged our rapture
know the fruit, make them swell with pus
choke on the abundance of ravished trees
and thick brown cracked out water

ancestor—
i cannot deny that name
we are a woven piece
of divinity

i am their most indignant war cry
and together
we are many

we will never
come kindly
we will lift
our blood
skin
breath
and hands
in union
to make this earth shake
and testify our name

this is harvest time.

{ libation }

the praying golden comfort hands hum sweet
come here melodic cries to god, with thirst
pulsing from their swollen shut throats
kicking over bloody populous trees
magnolia hushed colored rainbows dipped
on bended knee, the baddest black gospel
womyn. one day the seeds will know the wombs
that birthed their lives into pastures of free
endless springs. they'll hold freedom tightly
around their belly, forging blistered shut mouths
into hopeful entrenched libations.

{ roots }

i'm runnin' on—
renascence summer daze
past honey covered faces, lost somewhere
caught my reflection in a moonlit smoke
saw dreamy day eyes questioning freedom
brown brilliance wrapped up in melodic dream clothes

        i'm carrying the muster of alice and nina simone
        i am the buck black unicorn that the lorde rose,
            my coarse eyes audacious
            my bridged back, collapsed—

        i am
        sequoia long trees
      a wind that speaks gospel—
      i'm straddlin' earthquakes
       of broken love notes
     from black mama's hollowed cries
      their tears turned moonshine,
    choked down into the bloated bellies
      of fathers two-steppin' down
       blood-soaked dirt roads

gravel clogged and splattered
from white spittin' toothless men,
their low open pants
black-womyn-snatchin' hands, sullied
raping and thieving with a baby black boy hangin' in the yard

(or shot in the yard, or stabbed in the yard, or choked)

                                          i'm here
stretched from cement lined wombs
rising from gluttonous graveyards
cried out like the rocks
my hands open to god
i'm mystifying magic,
eradicating desolation
enchanted

i come
from chiseled mournings,
prayer hands at daybreak
and the wisdom of sunday afternoon

i am
the soul of black ladies hummin'
on sun dipped porches
wavin' away their desert dry tears,
chorused together in strong song
letting their calloused feet and soft dresses
show them vulnerable

i stand here
lookin' at the benevolent blackness of my inward self
ripe and reaching

{ fire at massa's house }

i am nakedly loud-toeing across galaxies
as worlds firework underneath my feet

i am kindling pluto's fire
with the fabric of my flesh
offering hands, mouth, and skin
all of my marrow as tinder

broken bones, hung necks, and worn hands
submerge eagerly into the fire

this is called rebel,
these pieces of what was
are no longer tired

~~this ain't no prophecy~~
this is revelation

i am sober in this heat, stoic
wrists sore from knocking at massa's
house, forever long, with tools heavy
with the residue of snatched teeth
bent backs, blood

this ain't spirit murder
nor death by suffocation
this a restful sleep

this ain't no weary haint
this the ghost who found the truth

we have not died trying
we burn flourished in triumph
the bellow in our voice
has diminished jericho's walls
we have all fallen

this is freedom time.

{ possession }

dive in
full breath
black hair
skin, teeth
stars all over
my damned belly
i'm bending blackness
collapsing into sweaty pools of
"don't tell nobody"
circles,
heaps of homoerotic healing
i'm reaching
cutting off whole massacres
from my scalp
creating poetry in response
choired together sounds
of deliberate quaking
oh, "we've all come this far by faith"
breathe
tell mama i'm coming back now
tell her i spoke my incantations to the sky
"how ever much you carry, you can always hold more," she say
i am always left to carry more

this poetry feel like deep drumming fists
it make my head on fire

i've been here in this place before

but i haven't ever touched it
let my breast out
give my cry some air to breathe
let me reach back into me
tongue and teeth back into me
bones and flesh back into me

i am folding myself unconscious

to give my back sweat a laugh
from all this carry
from all this shit we carry—
we are brown bodies fulfilling our own cravings
we push palms flat
slipping on the saltiness of our own sweat
our knees bow down
to the crowns of our own heads
divinely favoring ourselves
i feel it again,
the presences of knowing myself

i was not myself for weeks yet nobody noticed

i didn't notice, nor tell the truth
and reach my tongue
back into me

we have always been possessed
we speak, we move, we live through
so much struggle
we will ourselves too

we have always been light

ultra-light beaming
moving out of forever
surrendering to millenniums
of unknown space and time

i lay here delivered from evil
still feasting on unholy blood
stretched out in erotic space
shift-shaping
calling
"bring yourself here, fool"

when i try to be someone
i am not, my heart is
dissatisfied

{ rumble }

i wrestled myself here,

with black girl round thighs and dark knees.

jumped and swam with tired arms and broken legs

till i found my tongue swinging love notes

out from the back of my throat,

praying praises and good sweet thanks

to the kindness of the breeze.

{ loud mouth }

out of the center of my heart
i push out tongue, mouth, truth,
and the lies between my teeth
'till all of me just comes fallin' out
just comes bellowin'
in a loud cry i won't apologize for.

i speak with the fullness of that bitter
i once swallowed down
to preserve your feelings—
i laugh gangly and without remorse
i speak with virtue
wet and rumbly
like tough waters
and quiet tears

i sing off key until my heart is content
i chew on words
spit them out 'till i become belligerent,
i call myself silk
and i rain dance coolly
atop the secrets i know you want to share with me—

sometimes my lips spread madness
to be delivered from mundane shit
like overplayed love songs
and the world's rhythm spinnin' out of tune

often i hum to myself methodically,
to bring myself some company

my words come raspy and delivered
righteous and cloaked
come shoutin' in strung with love notes

my words are my deepest fear
my truth thought out
loud

like summer's rain,

quick
hot
magic

{ a first time }

and it felt good too

the day i learned how to touch myself
was the sweetest day of my lived life
i will never master this touch,
i am growing womyn
....

i make love to myself, often
i lace my hands into myself and twitch
my thighs grind until they rumble

dying to satisfy
desperate to quench

i dive my head back
my eyes roll into romance
i am everywhere
and become delight

i lick and sweat

my tongue even quivers
and smacks at this
goodness, we fuckin'

i become us and we and i
are up on our knees
rockin' our *sweet* pussy
back

and forth
hovering dizzily
climbing
pushing
until
it all comes

out

{ and the godly ones will hear us }

i want to write
poetry
on your back
tickle the flowerbeds
of your skin
i want to lick the salt
from inside you
spread your maple oaks
open
i want to pull myself into you
swim you to the top of
your mountain's
peak, lay with you
in eden
in her fullness
her thickness
her warm
black
beauty
spread your fragrance
on my butter tip nose
and i'll simmer
my womyn will
reign
a chocolate thunder
as tides
melt into
my mouth
i'll grow patient
as you push out

                                your womb
                     towards infinite skies
                              and freedom

                             you'll hum out
                             cathedral loud

~~love as long as the reach of the sequoia trees~~
{ reaching }

we were
two black
lady bird songs
stuck in high tunes
a wet-lipped melody
wanting love
chorused over ma rainey's blues,
the day that the lorde rose

I.

i miss you.

we've been distant lovers strung together in a space that knows no time. we've smooth danced through rainstorms and got lost together in words that made our hurt heal faster. our stories wrapped by each other finally felt like empathy.

i offered you words of audre, my street blood, my warrior wounds, my tender.

you gifted songs of compassion, some you didn't even know you had, songs of a caged bird, a freedom pass survival song, a chorus of longing lips.

i wanted us to rock together

under the thick air of nina's baritone gently beating over our backs,
as we took solace in kissing another soul
that finally shared our own language.

II.

we laughed in pirouettes around the sun
sat with our necks stretched up towards high clouds
aching to exist in carefree black womyn laughter
with tenacious hearts and sweaty hands
we took a joint breath on a perched hill
in clear blue air, and fell in love.

III.

you asked if you could kiss me,
my childhood stutter came out because i had never once been asked
for my consent.

IV.

i slept warmed against the sweater you left,
danced my nose into your collar to sing in remembrance
willingly eased my body into your spirit, my first time beginning to
love you pass your flesh.

V.

one high noon we sat fresh out the shower naked against our hand-picked bed of flowers. our bellies stretched with endless laughter. we yelped in sanctuary seconding each other's stories of white folk causing havoc. we swam in each other's past and found ourselves hurt by the same icebergs.

VI.

i remember the first time i cried for you.
nina sang "wild as the wind" on the record player,
our bed of flowers wilted surrounded by packed bags and empty
bottles of sangria.

i sat in my morning shower bellowing out my tears in my private
rainstorm, hoping you would hear my weepy eyes wanting you to stay.

VII.

often my mind stretches back to the day you cried on my brown breast,
in agony. we hadn't been flesh-to-flesh in so long. i drank the woodsy
smell of your melted skin and walked my fingertips through your curls.
you always loved when i swam in your hair. i savored watching every
part of our beings grow together, skin, soul, bone, and hair.

VIII.

sometimes i still laugh out loud to myself for pretending to know about
basketball. eagerly i watched your games on livestream, made notes of
rebounds and free throws, wrote them down like love poems, to soon
charm you with them later. over the phone or across the internet, our
laughter became distant.

IX.

no one ever tells you how hard it is to date another activist. muzzled by
cheers for revolutionary love, we were afraid to admit that we felt the
burns of each other's oppression in the blisters of our own skin.
we could touch each other's exile,
we burnt together.

X.

we had really great sex. but sometimes i wanted to craft. but three days of flesh time didn't always have room for sex, fighting, laughter, and crafting. crafting was always last on your to-do list but first on mine.

XI.

i've never met another soul who has made me feel as intelligent as you do. never once ridiculing me for my stutter, mispronunciations, or endless misspelled words. this to you, only made me smarter. you said my mind was flourishing with too many ways to teach people how to love that i didn't have time to correct misspelled words. when i said i could never teach because of a disability i didn't yet have a name for, you told me i was already a teacher.

XII.

i held my breath when i texted you that i was moving further away from you. i laid hidden between my blankets, craving your scent, and waited for the flood.

XIII.

i could feel your spirit wash away from the fabric of my bed sheets.

lost in a fog of you,
restless in time,
swallowed by space,
i miss sitting in clouds with you.

XIV.

i began to resent you. i knew what you were afraid of, but it always annoyed me how scary you were. why couldn't you just lace up a pair of combat boots and run into somewhere with me, push past space and time hand in hand and wonder into uncertainty.

XV.

a dear friend came over the night i halfheartedly decided to say goodbye to you. we made ice cream sandwiches while i cried cold tears and looked up sad music videos to get lost in. i wanted to know that someone else was in pain.

my dear friend held me while i faded into tired tears, in my sleep i thought she was you.

i don't know how to get you out of my dreams.

XVI.

through my suffering, i've learned from you that love is not the equivalent of commitment.

XVII.

i wish i would have titled this poem reaching. i have stretched my soul to you, extended myself through miles and minutes to grasp our love. i don't know how to draw myself back in now. i'm afraid that you and i will always be reaching.

XVIII.

i still believe that what we had was important.
i pray that time and space apologize to us.

{ spirit of discernment }

ain't nothing about this accidental
we didn't just come this far by grace
this is a practiced love
this is a conjured space

ain't nothing about this coincidental
we didn't just trip and fall
we dug and peeled and rinsed and rubbed
we committed to this haul

ain't nothing about this blind
it ain't reduced or refined
it's a hope named everlasting
a constant flow of time

{ loose womyn }

our souls knew each other
before we did
someplace magic
where thick cerulean silks
sprang from morning trees to greet us

our hot watery
brown bones broke
through the thickness of our sycamore covered skin
to be there

sometimes i sit on sunflower coated dreams
holding up my head to the skies
daring myself to witness
your hold-me-still eyes

most times my belly sits
tight, practicing heartbreak
because magic is for loose womyn
and witches and them ungodly folk
the worldly ones with lipstick stains
on their liberated blistered mouths—
plus my mother said i could never
should never, love this way

one day i pictured us naked
often we are naked
with our bloomers snatched

our pelvis up
and our breast erect towards a moonlight
we could barely make out
yet wanted so badly to feel

we daydreamed hopelessly
under ginkgo trees
tasted elderberry sweetness
on our black delicious mouths
juices thick and untouched
berries plucked from the finest fiery bush

we heard god there,
the one them godly ones can't hear
and collectively we reigned
above the glare of too much love lost
like a heaping explosive love machine
made of wet dreams, escape, and one-way ticket
train rides

{ time }

i need time to—
return
deliberate
decide
meditate
meddle
to breathe
capture
let go
descend
to think
and figure out
my shit,
alone.

{ wet behind the ears }

take me to the water,
take me to the water,
take me to the water,
to be baptized

age 8

mama is fresh. breast squeezed under a wool crisp suit framin' her face like chipped chocolate, only showin' the godly parts of herself. sunday's best got me itchin' from wool dresses and hot combed hair that don't feel like mine. last night i had my real clothes on, perched between the brown parts of mama's legs that don't show in church. mama had the wooden wide-tooth comb out, you know the one that supposed to lessen the pain of her rippin' through my hair and stressin' out my scalp. she was tryin' to get my deviant hair to fold down like the little white girl's hair do on tv because i was getting baptized tomorrow, and she wouldn't have my erect hair standin' up to god.

drop down turn around pick a bale of cotton
drop down turn around pick a bale of hay
oh lordy

age 10

mama got me wrapped up in some african cloth and i don't know where it's from, but it's african sunday at church even though i don't feel african. all i know is that little brown big-bone girls like me are supposed to be beautiful in africa. but we live around people from india and i go to school with white folk. you know, them folks my mama want my hair to look like. she claims she don't like them people forreal though. anyhow, them white folks and indians don't never speak beauty in my name, they only shout bastard and ugly at me. some of them africans do it too.

i got a father though. he just died early.

the angels bow down at the thought of you,
the darkness gives way to the light for you
the price that you paid gives us life brand new
hosanna forever we worship you

age 12

i remember being about twelve years old with ashy elbows and unpainted toes. staring at this big grotesque picture in our living room. it was a painting of the last supper, the black edition. all of the men had real big afros, even jesus himself. mama ain't never let us hang up no white folk, couldn't never have no white dolls neither. that big grotesque painting of black jesus and his fearful army stayed hug high in our home for years and it scared me shitless.

it was the same fear i had when i was left in the sanctuary alone at night after choir rehearsal or usher practice or bible study or drill team. there was always something that had me bone stiff in the middle of the sanctuary, quiet and scared.

hush, hush. somebody's callin' my name,
oh, my lord, oh, my lord, what shall i do?

age 13

i started seeing things real young. started seeing things float on pass me, hear things with no flesh. i didn't ask questions though, because my mama forbid me from talking about ghosts or the dead after daddy died. so i assumed that i was seeing demons because that was the only thing without flesh that mama still saw, still talked about.

all of them demons, crosses, and pictures of black jesus made me feel like i was being watched.

i grew guilty and terrified under that watch.

we've come this far by faith
leaning on the lord
trusting in his holy word
he hasn't failed me yet

age 16

as soon as i was of the mind to do it, i ran from god, and mama, and everything that looked like memory. i closed my ears from the sound of her hummin' her voice across down-home stickiness and up north depression.

one day i sat across from mama at a dinner table and told her that i thought jesus was a metaphor. told her i believed that there were many who lived the light of christ, bestowed that kind of justice. i was startin' to see the divinity within myself and i couldn't understand the notion of a god that wanted me to feel small and minimal.

i told the storm
to past, storm you can't last

go away, i demand you to move today

age 18

i've learned that sometimes god takes away everything you think you need on purpose. makes you fall down and fumble to your knees scrapin' with worn hands and a desolate throat 'till you ain't got no choice but to shout, no choice but to declare that i am made of earth and divinity god rules in me.

therefore i am magic
spellbound fortitude
the embodiment of creation

but mama always did say a hard head make a soft ass so i ain't learn this no easy way.

sister,
you've been on my mind
sister, we're two of a kind
so sister,
i'm keepin' my eyes on you

age 21

i remember reading *the color purple* for the first time and feelin' like everything that was green and beautiful and alive was speakin' to me. tellin' me to be sexy and sensual. to open myself, spread myself, to let go and let in.

so well, i even let in the bullshit, fucked it and craved it too. partially overcompensating for the parts of me that still thought that fat girls, and black girls, and queer girls were never promised love. back when i thought that love was supposed to be a whirlwind, a show, progress without exchange.

i loved recklessly. nailed my love on the walls of lovers who told me that it was unwanted. convinced that i could show up and show out until they decided to return my abundance. drunk, smoke, and abused my psych meds; i was willing to do anything to actualize my fantasies and live the story of love i just knew them skinny bitches was livin'.

i was still going to war with god, dueling with myself, squeezing and stuffin' and compromising my juicy ass to fit into a world built on soil suffocated by thorns.

sometimes you have to encourage yourself
sometimes you have to speak victory during the test

age 22

at twenty-two i remembered that i was small, a living thing, wet behind the ears. i stuck my neck out to hide my bluff. i wanted to be anything but vulnerable. everything that looked like a rising star, or like glory. i thought that if i hung with all the right crowds, even though they didn't favor me, that surely i would reap reverence and splendor. because surely i had already endured enough suffering, amassed enough heartbreak. more prodigal like than i knew, i found myself humbled in the arms of god.

woke up with this morning with my mind set on loving me
with my mind set on loving me
i'm not lonely, i'm alone
and i'm holy by my own

age 25

with memories dyed into my skin
and wander laced around my feet,
i've learned that freedom is a moving thing.

i've learned that peace is faith in change.

i am fire, heat is all up through me, i know that i am a tempered thing.

i am willing. ready to greet the sun. i am humbled and rescued, counting on the moon. walking with steady feet to the river to lay all this shit down.

i am sitting in discomfort, in pain, in uncertainty. allowing it to move through me, allowing it to pass. i have wept for so long.

now i nourish my body with honey, cover her in gemstones, stretch me into space. now i covet joy.

hallowed be thy name thy kingdom come,
work through me and with me, thy will be done.

i am learning purpose.
bounty after sacrifice.
a deliverance that does not seize.

a glorious type of faith.

{ notes }

psalms 23 (king james version)

"wet behind the ears" incorporates language from the following:

    wade in the water (negro spiritual)

    pick a bale of cotton by lead belly

    hosana by kirk franklin

    we've come this far by faith by albert goodson

    i told the storm by greg o'quin 'n joyful noize

    miss celie's blues by quincy jones

    encourage yourself by donald lawrence

    holy by jamila woods

Thank You

This creation would not be possible without my beloved mama and daddy and my righteous ancestors. To my mama, thank you for teaching me to know God. I am the consequence of your faith. To my daddy, thank you for teaching me the power of loving after death. I carry both your compassion and your hustle. To my ancestors, thank you for persistently making it clear what kind of matter I'm made of. To my spirit led family, thank you for loving me in my difference and defiance. Thank you for praying for me without seize.

I have a whole heap of gratitude planted inside of me for all the incredible writers, friends, lovers, and loved ones who have had any part in helping me release this collection into the world. Mary, Rikki, Jeff, Ebony, thank you for seeing power and healing in my words. Sabrina, Megan, Jenni, Shannan, Simone, Molly, Chloe, Asia, Erefaka, and the many others who have blessed me, thank you for being a friend to my mind and a ram in the bush. I am forever grateful for your love.

To my sister-friend Marche, thank you for being a constant encourager and seeing me as a writer in times when I couldn't realize it for myself. You have stood in the gap for me.

To the innumerable water spirits that have held my body and washed away my grief, I am humbled and grateful to be your child. I pray you continue to groom me.

To our beloved Toni, thank you for existing. I am because you are.

To our immaculate God, thank you for favoring me and ordering my steps. Thank you for extending me comfort and joy in the midst of many dark and desperate nights. What an honor it is to be a child of the great divine.

The Author

Originally from Chicago, Naomi Scherelle Daugherty is a writer, cartomancer, educator, and alchemist currently cultivating liberation for Black folks in the holy city of New Orleans. Naomi has spent her time in education teaching high school students how to read, write, hustle, and heal themselves. In 2014, her poem "I hate being called a lesbian" was published by Blackberry: A Magazine. In 2015, two of Naomi's poems were published by RaedLeaf Poetry alongside the work of Monica Hand. In 2016, Naomi co-founded 4ColouredGurlz, a wholistic wellness business that is an ode to Black folks and a declaration that all oppressed bodies are due comfort and joy. As a cartomancer, Naomi spends much of her time watching fire burn and facilitating a word for those in need. *The Clearing* is Naomi's first published collection of poetry.

www.ingramcontent.com/pod-product-compliance
Lightning Source LLC
Chambersburg PA
CBHW030916170426
43193CB00009BA/878